Did you hear about the Italian
who cleaned his ears?
His head caved in.

*   *   *

One guy said to the other guy,
"Hey, I like your shoes. What kind
are they?"
His friend replied,
"They're my Italian shoes."
"Italian shoes?"
"Yeah. Wherever I go, Dago."

*   *   *

Why does the new Italian navy
have glass-bottomed boats?
So they can see the old Italian navy.

500 GREAT
ITALIAN
JOKES

BY

JAY ALLEN

Ⓢ

A SIGNET BOOK

NEW AMERICAN LIBRARY

A DIVISION OF PENGUIN BOOKS USA INC.

Copyright © 1990 by Jay Allen

SIGNET, SIGNET CLASSIC, MENTOR, ONYX, PLUME, MERIDIAN
and NAL BOOKS are published by New American Library,
a division of Penguin Books USA Inc.,
1633 Broadway, New York, New York 10019

First Printing, February, 1990

1 2 3 4 5 6 7 8 9

PRINTED IN THE UNITED STATES OF AMERICA

CONTENTS

CHAPTER 1

GREAT ETHNIC INSULTS ABOUT ITALIANS

How do you recognize an Italian plane?
It's got hair under the wings.

How can you tell an Italian cesspool?
It's the one with the diving board.

What's the best-selling underarm deodorant in Italy?
Raid.

Why are rectal thermometers banned in Italy?
They caused too much brain damage.

Why won't there ever be an Italian president?
They'd never find enough plastic slipcovers for all the sofas in the White House.

Did you hear about the Italian businessman who went broke?
He imported 1 million cans of underarm deodorant into Italy and didn't sell a single one.

How do Italians count?
1, 2, 3, 4, 5, another, another, another, another . . .

Why do Italians and Jews get along?
Italians invented the toilet seat, Jews invented the hole.

Why don't Italians take showers?
Because oil and water don't mix.

What do you call an Italian who marries a black?
A social climber.

Why doesn't the navy let Italians join underwater demolition teams?
They leave oil slicks.

What do you call an Italian with half a brain?
Gifted.

What do you call an Italian woman who takes birth-control pills?
A humanitarian.

How do you recognize an Italian airliner?
It has outdoor toilets.

Why do flies have wings?
So they can beat Italians to the garbage cans.

What do you call a frozen cesspool?
Italian ice.

What's an upper-class Italian home?
One where the ashtrays don't have writing on them.

Why is it impossible to walk across Italy?
No one can hold his nose that long.

Two guys were walking down the street. One said to the other, "You know, I really hate Italians. Those greasy wops are so loud, their food reeks of garlic, and they'll steal you blind. I'd like to ship every single one back to Italy."

The other guy was about to comment when they rounded a corner. But he stopped as he saw an organ grinder belting out "O Solo Mio" at the top of his lungs. The guy was still gawking when, to his amazement, his friend reaches in his pocket, pulls out a five-dollar bill, and gives it to the organ grinder's monkey.

"Jesus, Fred!" the guy exclaimed. "I thought you hated Italians?"

"I do," Fred replied. "But those young ones are so cute!"

Why is Italy shaped like a boot?
They couldn't fit all that shit into a sneaker.

A guy walks into a psychiatrist's office with a chicken on his head. The shrink asks, "What can I do for you?"

The chicken replies, "Get this greasy wop off my ass."

What do you get when you cross an Italian and a gorilla?
Nothing. A gorilla's too smart to fuck an Italian.

What's an Italian cocktail?
A glass of wine with a booger in it.

Why don't they let Italians swim in the Mediterranean?
Because they leave a ring.

Why don't Italians have freckles?
Because they slide off.

What do you call the brother of an Italian's mother?
A monkey's uncle.

Is it true that Italian fishermen can catch fish without a hook, bait, or net?
True. They drop their pants, lower their asses into the water, then fart. The fish jump into the boat.

Why did God give Italians arms?
So their fingers wouldn't smell like their armpits.

How do they make Italian sausage?
From retarded pigs.

Why do Italians save the ring pulls off beer cans?
To use as nose pickers.

What's one advantage of being Italian?
You never miss a call because you're in the bathtub.

Did you hear about the Chinese-Italian restaurant?
Ah Fung Goo.

What's the national bird of Italy?
The guinea hen.

What's the national bird of Sicily?
The stool pigeon.

Two Italian women were talking excitedly about Frank Sinatra's upcoming concert in their city. One said to the other, "I'ma so excited. I think I'm gonna go to the airport to see him come in."

"How you gonna know which plane he's on?"

The first woman said, "I'll just go to the TWA gate and wait."

The second woman was puzzled. "How you know he's gonna fly TWA?"

"What do you think TWA stands for—Top Wop Aboard."

What do you call an Italian test-tube baby?
Janitor in a drum.

What do you get when you cross an Italian with a gorilla?
A grease monkey.

What's the fastest way to get your car lubed?
Run over an Italian.

Why are there so few Sicilians on the Italian Olympic team?
Donkey fucking isn't an Olympic sport.

What's an Italian Jacuzzi?
Farting in the bathtub.

How do Italian men put on their underwear?
Yellow in front, brown in the rear.

Did you hear that newspapers have changed the way they handle obituaries of Italians?
They're now listed under "Civic Improvements."

How can you tell if a guy in a bar is Italian?
When he smokes, he blows onion rings.

How can you tell if a guy is Italian?
Have him breathe on a vampire. If the vampire dies, the guy's Italian.

Why did the cannibal take a bite of shit?
He'd just eaten an Italian, and he was trying to get the taste out of his mouth.

Why don't they let Italian women swim in lakes?
Ten minutes after they jump in, the water's covered with dead fish.

How can you tell a guy in a singles bar is Italian?
His class ring is the pull top off a Budweiser can.

Why do Italians wear hats?
So they know which end to wipe.

Why do Italians use their fingers to pick their noses?
Because their tongues aren't long enough.

What do you call the index finger of a Italian's left hand?
A handkerchief.

Did you hear about the Italian who had an asshole transplant?
The asshole rejected him.

What do Italian mothers-in-law use as garter belts?
Inner tubes.

What's the primary advantage of being Italian?
You don't have to go to the zoo—the zoo comes and gets you.

If Tarzan and Jane were Italian, what would Cheetah be?
The least hairy of the three.

How do you keep Italians out of your front yard?
Keep your garbage cans out back.

Did you hear about the Italian who cleaned his ears?
His head caved in.

What's an Italian cocktail?
A meatball in a glass of wine.

Did you hear about the Italian who saved for years to buy his mother a house?
And when he bought it, the vice squad wouldn't let her run it.

What's the quickest way to find an Italian's fingerprints?
Look in his nose.

What's the difference between an Italian and a Pole?
The Pole takes the dishes out before he pisses in the sink.

What do flamingos do when they get married?
Buy two cast-iron Italians to put on the lawn.

What do you call a manhole cover in Washington, D.C.?
The front door to the Italian embassy.

Why do Italians talk with their hands?
Because they can't stand each other's breath.

Did you hear about the latest Italian medical breakthrough?
Perfecting the hemorrhoid transplant.

What's three miles long and has an IQ of 187?
The Columbus Day parade.

Did you hear that British naturalists uncovered some important footage from World War II?
The film showed three Italian birds surrendering to a worm.

Why does the new Italian navy have glass-bottom boats?
So they can see the old Italian navy.

Why did the Italian army form an attack force made up solely of epileptics?
So the enemy couldn't tell which ones had been shot.

How can you sink an Italian submarine?
Put it in the water.

How can you tell an Italian army tank?
It's the one with backup lights.

Why do Italian army surplus weapons command such a stiff price?
They've never been fired.

Why didn't the Italian air force bomb England during World War II?
The rubber bands broke before they got to the Channel.

What's the first piece of equipment issued to an Italian soldier?
A white flag.

What's the thinnest book in the world?
Italian War Heros.

How do you sink an Italian submarine?
Knock on the door.

Who really assassinated President John F. Kennedy?
Five hundred Italian sharpshooters.

How can you tell an Italian firing squad?
They're the ones standing in a circle.

What do they call an Italian admiral?
Chicken of the Sea.

Why don't Italian sailors need lifeboats?
Oil floats.

How do you train Italians to be soldiers?
First, teach them how to put their hands in the air.

Why are all Italian soldiers considered linguists?
They know how to say "I surrender" in 57 languages.

What happened in the Middle East when Iran attacked Iraq?
An hour later, Italy surrendered.

Why are there no Italian paratroopers?
No Italian can count to ten.

Why are there screen doors on Italian submarines?
To keep fish out.

CHAPTER 2

GREAT JOKES ABOUT THE SEX LIVES OF ITALIANS

"Come on," Mario said to his friend. "Why don't you take out my cousin? She's a real girl-next-door type."

"Right," his friend said. "If you live next door to the zoo."

Luigi finally managed to get the attention of the gorgeous blonde at the bar. After a few drinks, she got very friendly. Finally, she leaned over to him and whispered, "The one thing I'm looking for is a man who can really deliver."

So Luigi went out and brought her back a pizza.

How do you recondition an old Italian whore? Shove a ten-pound ham up her twat and pull out the bone.

The guy had a fetish for hairy women, so when he saw the Italian lady with the dark mustache sitting on a bar stool, he knew it was true love. After he bought her several drinks, they went back to her apartment. When she took off her blouse, he was thrilled to see that she had huge growths under her armpits. He ran his hands through the hair as she took off her panties, then turned his attention to her fabulous bush.

She watched him, then said, "Listen, mac. I brought you here to fuck, not to knit."

The Italian girl finally admitted to her mother that she was pregnant.

The mother asked, "Are you sure it's yours?"

Why did the Italian girl get pregnant?
She fed her birth-control pills to storks.

How can an Italian man tell when his wife is having an orgasm?
An Italian man doesn't care.

The Italian couple asked their oldest kid what he wanted for his birthday. He replied, "I wanna watch."

So they let him.

Why do Italian women prefer screwing to bowling? The balls are lighter and you don't need special shoes.

Why do old women love young Italian guys? Italians will eat anything.

Did you hear about the new Italian designer condoms?
They're called Sergio Prevente.

Why did the Italian salesman quit his job? His boss gave him virgin territory.

The young Sicilian farmer was called in by the authorities to take a blood test to determine if he was the father of a baby born to a farm girl who had been raped. He was white with fear when he took the test, but his friends were amazed to see him swagger confidently out of the hospital.

"The test was negative?" one friend asked.

"The results aren't back yet," the Sicilian replied. "But there's no way they'll get me. That stupid doctor took the sample from my finger."

The young Italian fruit peddler knocked on the front door and asked the shapely housewife if she wanted to buy some strawberries. The woman asked him to come around to the back door. When he got to the rear of the house, he saw the woman standing just inside the screen door, stark naked. Immediately, the young Italian started to sob uncontrollably.

Stunned, the woman asked him what was wrong.

"A month ago, my mama and papa, they died," he replied. "Three weeks ago, my wife ran off with my partner. Two weeks ago, my store burned to the ground. Last week my dog got run over by a truck. And now," he continued, "I'm just about to be fucked out of my last strawberries."

While visiting the United States, the Italian girl ran out of money just before her visa expired. She was in despair until she ran into a sailor who told her he'd smuggle her aboard his ship and bring her food during the voyage. All she had to do in return was provide sexual services. Desperate, the girl agreed.

Late that night, the sailor sneaked her aboard the vessel, and twice each day afterward he brought her food and reaped his reward. Finally, after two weeks, the captain became suspicious and followed the sailor. He witnessed the bartering, then confronted the girl.

She told him the whole story. He mused for a moment, then said, "Hum, rather clever of the young man. However, miss, it's only fair to tell you that this is the Staten Island Ferry."

Why did the young Italian girl fail her driver's test?
Every time the car stopped, she jumped into the backseat.

Did you hear about the Italian who went to visit his cousin and discovered she didn't have any clothes on?
Nine months later, he visited her again and discovered she had a little moron.

Did you hear about the Italian abortion service that makes house calls?
It's called Roto-Rootor.

Why are Italian hookers so busy?
They never let a dago by.

Why is an Italian girl like a doorknob?
Everybody gets a turn.

Did you hear that the Italian airline Alitalia just merged with General Mills?
The new company's called Genitalia.

The Mafia big shot arrived at the party, and heads turned as he walked into the room surrounded by bodyguards. The gorgeous blonde was very impressed. Soon, she caught the don's eye, and they got into an intimate conversation.

An hour later, the blonde and the mobster were

in a suite at a posh midtown hotel. The don took off his clothes. To the intense disappointment of the blonde, his dick was about an inch long. "Just who do you expect to please with that?" she scoffed.

"Me," he replied.

The psychotic killer knew that the American police were hot on his trail, so he hopped a plane to Italy and made his way to a small town on the Mediterranean. For a few weeks he was able to restrain himself. Finally, he went out into the streets in the wee hours of the morning, found a hooker, lured her into an alley, slashed her throat, then sated himself as her vital fluid gushed out of her body. When he was done, he dragged the corpse to the docks and tossed it into the sea.

The next morning, ravaged with guilt, he vowed never to do it again. But in a few days he was back on the streets and sated himself once more. Then he killed again a week later, and a fourth time.

Because the disappearances were beginning to be a topic of conversation in the small town, the psycho was particularly alert when he dragged the body of his fifth victim to the sea. He tossed her into the wine-dark water, then listened carefully. A moment later, to his surprise, he saw a shark rise up to grab the corpse, then heard it sing, "Drained wops keep falling on my head. . . ."

What's the difference between a screen door and an Italian girl?
A screen door stops squealing when you lubricate it.

What does a Sicilian girl do after she sucks cock?
Spits out the feathers.

The Italian parents were worried about their daughter Angela, who had started to date a waiter at the local pizza joint. Every night she went out with him after work, only to come home disheveled in the wee hours of the morning.

Finally, her mother went to her and said, "Angela, Papa and I are so worried about you and this Mario kid. Is he gonna marry you? What are his intentions?"

"I don't know, Mama," the girl replied. "He keeps me pretty much in the dark."

The Sicilian girl's parents still believed in arranged marriages. They never let her out without a chaperon until they arranged a match with the son of a wealthy wine merchant. The girl was pleased when a presentable-looking young man picked her up for her first date. But she was seething with anger when she got back home a few hours later.

"What'sa matter?" her mother asked.

"That jerk!" she exclaimed. "He took me for a ride in his car, and I hadda slap him three times."

"To keep his hands off you?" her mother asked.

"To wake him up!"

The young Olympic swimming champion was vacationing in Rome when he met a stunning Italian girl. He wined and dined her for days, taking her to the most expensive places in town. Finally, in a final attempt to dazzle her, he led her to a table by the swimming pool at his hotel, recruited a waiter to hold a stopwatch, jumped in the water, and proceeded to swim 400 meters in world record time.

When he caught his breath, he went up to her and said, "Well, what do you think?"

Without a word, she arose, signaled the time, then dived into the water. To his utter astonishment, she bested his time. When she came back to the table, he sputtered, "Darling, I didn't know you were a champion swimmer, too."

"I'm not," she replied. "Before I came to Rome, I was a streetwalker in Venice."

Angelo was pacing in the waiting room with another guy. The other guy finally said, "I can't believe the bad luck. I'm on vacation this week."

"You think you've got bad luck," Angelo replied. "I'm on my honeymoon."

What's the most common Italian wedding proposal?
"You're what?"

The couple was going at it hot and heavy in the backseat of the car when the girl asked, "Angelo, will you love me like this after we're married?"

"Sure," the young tough replied. "I always liked married broads."

Why did the Italian girl buy a circular bed?
She decided she wanted to sleep around.

When did the Italian stud realize he'd been sleepwalking?
He woke up in his own bed.

Why is a horny Italian guy like a homicide detective?
They're both crack investigators.

Angelo was admitted to the hospital for emergency plastic surgery on his penis. After he came to, the surgeon asked him how he'd suffered the injury.

"Well," he began, "I live in a camper, and right next door is a camper that belongs to this beautiful blonde. I couldn't help peeping through the windows, and I discovered that every night before bed she sticks a sausage in a hole in the floor, takes off her clothes, and starts fucking it. I couldn't resist, so one night I crawled under the camper and stuck my dick up in through the hole where the sausage goes. I'm having a great time. Then someone knocked on the door and she tried to kick the sausage under the stove."

An Italian guy walked into one of his hangouts to find a beautiful girl he'd dated before sitting in a booth, weeping over a brandy. He sat down opposite her and asked, "Maria, what's wrong?"

"Everything," she sobbed. "My parents were killed in an car accident, I was fired from my job, I'm being evicted from my apartment, and I discovered I have fatal cancer."

"That's terrible," he said consolingly. "What

about if I take you out Saturday night and cheer you up?"

She shook her head no. "I've decided to kill myself Saturday night."

The Italian guy shrugged. "Well, what about Friday night?"

How can a good, Catholic Italian girl avoid pregnancy?
She just has to use her head.

What do Italian men do if their girlfriends are slow learning about sex?
Just pound it into their heads.

Did you hear about the Italian girl who said she'd do anything for a fur coat?
Now she can't button it over her belly.

An obnoxious young Italian guy walked up to a young lady sitting at the bar, leered, then said, "Hey, gorgeous, I'd love to get into those pants of yours."

"No way," the woman said dryly. "One asshole in there is enough."

An Italian guy walked up to a girl on the street and asked, "Hey, babe, what do you say to some ass?"

"Hello, ass," she replied, walking away.

What's "gentlemanly?"
The way an Italian guy treats a woman he hasn't fucked yet.

What did the Italian girl say when the dog licked her belly?
"Down, boy."

Why did the Italian guy screw his sister-in-law?
He had it in for his brother.

The Italian guy arrived in the whorehouse. The red light in the window had been turned off, but he was so horny that he knocked and knocked and knocked. Finally, the angry madam stuck her head out an upper-floor window and shouted, "Stop that racket. We're closed for the day."

The Italian guy pleaded, "I got a problem. What should I do?"

"Beat it," she replied.

Why are Italian girls so good at oral sex?
They practice eating spaghetti with their hands tied behind their back.

What's the difference between an Italian guy and a pig?
A pig won't stay in a bar all night trying to fuck an Italian.

How do Italian women hold their liquor?
By the ears.

What's the definition of a perfect Italian woman?
A blind, deaf, and dumb nymphomaniac whose father owns a vineyard.

What positions do most Italian men like to screw in?
"POSITIONS?"

The Italian deli owner's daughter was fast becoming an old maid. She'd turned thirty, and she refused to date, causing her father no end of worry.

One night, however, the deli owner heard his daughter sneak out of her room. He got up and followed her downstairs, hoping she was meeting a man. Instead, he saw her masturbating furiously with a piece of sausage from the meat case.

The next day, the father was behind the counter when a customer pointed to the bratworst and asked, "How much is that?"

The owner grunted, then replied. "That's not for sale. That's my son-in-law."

Why did the Italian girl have her zip code tattooed on her thighs?
She hoped to get some male in her box.

Where do Italian hookers work?
Doghouses.

What's the worst thing about dating a fat Italian girl?
When she sits on your face, you can't hear the stereo.

Did you hear about the ugly Italian guy who finally turned to wine as a substitute for women?
He got his dick caught in the mouth of the bottle.

Why did the Italian guy put a quarter in his condom?
So if he couldn't come, he could call.

Why do old Italian women wear black garters?
In memory of those who have passed beyond.

The Italian had just been introduced to his date, and they started to dance. Suddenly the guinea thrust his hand into her pants and shoved a finger up her ass.

Startled and angry, the woman jumped back and yelled, "Gross."

So the Italian guy did it 143 more times.

What's another name for Italian prostitutes?
Guinea pigs.

What's the difference between a Jewish American Princess and an Italian American Princess?
With an Italian American Princess, the jewels are fake and the orgasms are real.

The rookie on the police force was sitting on a stool in the local hangout after his first day on patrol. His partner, a veteran, had spent the day introducing him to people on his beat. The two were on their second beers when a gorgeous, stacked young Italian chick walked into the bar.

"Wow," the rookie exclaimed. He turned to his partner and asked, "Who is that?"

"I don't know her real name," the partner replied. "Everybody refers to her as 911."

"As 911? What does that mean?"

"Every time she gets a call, a cop comes."

The Italian stud walked into the bar looking like he'd been run over by a truck. His hair was matted, his face bloody and scratched, his clothes torn. His friends bought him a beer, then asked, "What happened?"

The guy chugged the beer and said, "I was fighting for Angela Martelli's virginity?"

"No kidding?"

"Yeah. But that little bitch wouldn't let it go."

Why is an Italian man like a microwave oven? They both heat up instantly, then go "ding" in twenty seconds.

How do you know your Italian date is really ugly? When you get a ticket for violating the leash law.

What's an Italian husband's idea of fast talking?
Coming home from a date at three A.M. and convincing his wife his breath smells because he had tuna for dinner.

Why was the Italian guy so horny when he came home from Las Vegas?
He'd lost all his fucking money.

The young woman arrived at her new job, and the boss told her, "We'll expect you to do the same thing here as you did on your last job, Miss Carlucci."

"I don't mind," the young Italian girl said, "as long as you don't insist that I have to swallow that stuff."

Did you hear about the Italian hooker who mistakenly scheduled two johns for the same time?
She managed to squeeze both of them in.

Vito's life had been miserable since he was a small boy because he was the skinniest kid in Little Italy. All during his teenage years, the other kids teased him and called him names. Finally, it was his twenty-first birthday and he'd never even had a date. To drown his sorrows, he stopped by a local bar for a glass of wine.

To his amazement, a very well-built, young divorcée sidled over to him, started up a conversation, bought him a drink, then said, "What you say, should we go back to my place?"

Vito was so excited he could hardly walk. He followed the woman to her apartment. She pointed to the bedroom, then said, "Take off all your clothes and get into bed."

Vito did as he was told and lay shivering with excitement under the covers. Then the door opened. The woman came in with a seven-year-old boy, turned on the lights, pulled down the covers, and said, "See, Rocco. You don't eat your spaghetti and that's what you're gonna look like."

How does a gynecologist tell if an Italian patient is a hooker?
When she insists that he undress first.

The Italian father waited up one night for his daughter. When she walked in at three A.M., he was furious. He told her, "I told you that Mario is no good. You gotta stop seeing him."

"But Papa," she protested. "Mario treats me good. And he makes me healthy."

"How can he make you healthy?"

"You know how I used to bleed once a month? Well, he cured me."

What did the Italian starlet have tattooed on her back?

"Made in Hollywood—by almost everyone."

After the wedding, the Italian bride went to the upstairs bedroom with the groom while her mama stayed in the kitchen cooking the lasagne. A few minutes later, the young girl appeared in the kitchen and said in a terrified voice, "Mama, he's got hair all over his chest."

Her mother said, "Sophia, that's normal. Go back upstairs and do your duty."

A few minutes later, the girl ran into the kitchen again, wailing, "Mama, Mama, he's got hair all over his legs."

Again, her mother said, "That's normal. Go back upstairs and do your duty."

The girl went back to her husband. The guy took off his shoes and socks. She saw that while one foot was normal, the other was a clubfoot.

Once again, she ran to the kitchen screaming, "Mama, Mama, he's got half a foot."

Her mother replied, "You stay here an' make the lasagna. I'll go upstairs."

A well-built young Italian girl walked into the jewelry store to look for earrings to match a stunning new diamond bracelet. The owner came over to help her. He examined the huge stones in the bracelet, then said, "Madam, I'm afraid I have some bad news. Those stones in your bracelet aren't real diamonds."

The Italian girl screamed, "Help, I've been raped!"

What's an anchovy?
A small fish that smells like a finger.

What do they call an Italian girl who keeps running away from home?
A virgin.

What did the Italian woman do when she heard there was a Peeping Tom in the neighborhood?
Washed every window twice.

Why do Italians screw at an angle?
They're wopsided.

Did you hear that two great things have come out of Italy in the last twenty years?
Sophia Loren has both of them.

The Italian guy escorted the young girl back to his apartment. While they were rolling in the sack, the girl said, "You know, you remind me of Don Juan."

The guy said, "The great lover? But isn't he dead?"

The girl said, "That's what I mean."

CHAPTER 3

GREAT JOKES ABOUT ITALIANS AND MARRIAGE

Maria fell madly in love with her dentist, and soon she enticed him into an affair. One day, however, the dentist said to her, "Maria, we have to stop seeing each other. I'm sure your husband's going to get suspicious."

"But why?" Maria asked. "We've been screwing for six months and he hasn't said a thing?"

"He will soon," the dentist replied. "You're down to one tooth."

Why is it cheaper to marry an Italian woman? She already has a fur coat.

The Italian immigrant went to the doctor to complain that he wasn't sure how to make his new wife pregnant. After struggling with language problems, the doctor simplified his advice—just stick your longest thing where your wife is the hairiest.

Two months later, the Italian came back to complain, "It donna work. I've been sticking my nose in her armpit every night, and nothing's a happened!"

The Italian man swept his young voluptuous bride away from the reception and up to the bedroom. Before she undressed, she turned to him shyly and said, "Now that we're married, can you show me what a penis is?"

Pleased that his wife was obviously a virgin, he dropped his pants. He let her stare for a moment, then he asked, "What do you think?"

She replied, "Well, it's just like a prick—only smaller."

Giuseppe became increasingly infuriated because his wife had a headache every night. They fought loud enough to wake the neighbors. So it was a real surprise when he came home one night with a large, elaborately wrapped present.

"*Mama mia!*" she exclaimed. "Is this for me?"

He nodded.

She undid the wrapping and was stunned to find six live kittens. "Why kittens?" she asked.

Giuseppe grunted, then replied, "Six pallbearers for that dead pussy of yours."

A woman met her friend at the butcher's and exclaimed, "Gina, you look terrible! What's wrong?"

"It's Tony," she replied. "Every night, he's gotta sleep with his hand in my cunt."

"What's wrong with that?"

"He walks in his sleep."

The Italian couple's sex life was terrible, so they decided to go to France for a vacation. On the first day, they went to a little café and began talking to French couples, asking for suggestions. When they got back to the hotel, the husband said to the wife, "All right, I'll do it. I'll go down on you, like those Frenchmen do. But before I do, you gotta do something about that bad smell. Go to that shop they were talking about and buy some of that feminine deodorant spray."

The wife went out. When she returned, she was very excited. "You should see the flavors they have. Strawberry, chocolate, cherry, wine—"

The husband was starting to get excited, too. "That's terrific," he interrupted. "What flavor did you get?"

"Anchovy," she replied.

Did you hear about the Italian who believed in long engagements?
His girlfriend was six months pregnant when he married her.

What did the Sicilian father say when the young man announced he wanted to marry his daughter?
He was so surprised, the shotgun fell right out of his hands.

On the day before her twelfth baby was due, Mrs. Masucci told her husband, "I've had it. You men want more and more children, but now we women have fixed it. We went to the church and prayed to the saint to make the fathers share the pain of labor. And from the way the candles flared, I know the saint listened."

The husband laughed at her superstition. Later that night, Mrs. Masucci began to feel the first labor pains. Smugly, her husband touched his stomach. Nothing, not the least twinge. He leaned forward and poured himself another glass of wine.

Then, suddenly, from the street came a terrible scream. The man from next door was clutching his belly and rolling on the sidewalk. . . .

An Italian girl walked into the drugstore and asked the pharmacist what he recommended for her husband's dandruff. The pharmacist suggested Head & Shoulders.

Two days later the pharmacist received a call from the girl. "How do you give 'shoulders'?"

What's Italian birth control?
Kicking your husband in the shins to make him limp.

Did you hear about the Italian whose wife asked him to change his baby son?
He showed up two hours later with a baby girl.

What did the Italian guy do with his first fifty-cent piece?
He married her.

Why was the Italian housewife so pissed off when she heard her husband was out late shooting craps?
She didn't know how to cook them.

Why did the Italian take his pregnant wife to the pizza parlor?
Because they advertised "Free Delivery."

Why wouldn't the Italian guy go out with his wife?
Because she's a married woman.

The very virile young man arrived on the boat from Sicily and was greeted by his much older cousin and his wife. They took him back to their very small apartment. Since they had no guest room, they invited the young immigrant to share their bed.

The lights were turned off. The young man was about to fall asleep when he was jolted awake by a hand caressing his organ. Then the wife whispered in his ear, "Pluck a hair from my husband's ass. If he doesn't wake up, we can make love."

The young man did as directed, then proceeded to climb on top of the buxom wife and vigorously pump away. The experience was so fulfilling that they decided to follow the same procedure a second time, then a third.

Suddenly, the husband sat up in bed and said, "Giuseppe, I don't mind you screwing my wife. But do you have to use my ass as a scorecard?"

Why do Italian women marry Italian men?
Because vibrators don't buy furs and Cadillacs.

The Italian woman hauled her husband into court and told the judge, "You gotta give me a divorce."

The judge asked, "On what grounds?"

"Hobosexuality," the Italian woman replied.

The judge said, "Don't you mean homosexuality?"

"Nah, hobosexuality," she said. "He's a bum fuck."

Angelo lost his job when the bakery closed and spent the next two months looking for work. Finally, he came home one night with a monkey. Seeing his wife's astonished look, he explained, "I went over to my father's house and borrowed his old accordian. The chimp and me, we're gonna play on the street."

His wife said, "But what's that thing gonna eat?"

"He eats everything," the guy replied. "So we buy a couple extra bananas."

His wife grimaced. "But where does it go to the bathroom?"

"The monkey's trained to use the john, just like us."

The wife looked even more displeased. "So where's this ape gonna sleep."

"With us."

The wife looked disgusted. "But what about the smell?"

Angelo shrugged. "If I got used to it, so can the monkey."

What's the definition of an Italian wife?
An attachment you screw on the bed to get the housework done.

How fat are Italian wives?
They have to bat their eyelashes by hand.

Mrs. Ricci went to the doctor for her annual checkup. That night, when her husband arrived home, he found her preening in front of the mirror, squeezing her big tits. "What are you doing?" he asked.

She replied, "The doctor told me I have the breasts of an eighteen-year-old."

The husband grunted. "But what did the doc say about your fifty-five-year-old ass?"

She grimaced. "He didn't say anything about you."

A sex researcher knocked on the door of an Italian household and the husband answered. He agreed to be questioned about the sex life of himself and his wife. In response to the question "Frequency of intercourse?" he replied, "Twice a week."

"And for your wife?" the researcher asked. "Twice a week?"

"Nah," the man replied. "I'd say a dozen times a night."

"There must be some mistake," the researcher said.

The man shrugged. "No mistake. But it's only till we pay off the loan sharks."

The Italian man paced in the hospital waiting room, smoking cheap cigars and lunging for every nurse who walked through the room. When the man's wife finally gave birth, the nurses were so irritated that they decided to shake him up by bringing out a black baby to show him.

To their surprise, the Italian didn't react at all. Finally, one nurse asked, "What do you think?"

"Cute kid," the man said.

"Don't you think it's strange that the baby is black?"

"Nah," the guy replied, puffing on the cigar, "my wife burns everything."

An Italian man was sitting at the bar when his neighbor came up, sat down beside him, and asked, "Angelo, do you like a woman with a stomach big as a medicine ball?"

"No," Angelo replied.

"What about a woman with tits that sag all the way down to her knees?"

"No way."

"And what about one with a big hole that stinks like an outhouse?"

"Ugh!" Angelo said with disgust. "Why you asking me these stupid questions?"

"Just one reason," his neighbor replied. "I couldn't figure out why the hell you were screwing my wife."

Did you hear about the Italian couple who had a double-ring ceremony?
They were married in a bathtub.

Why didn't the Italian girl's mother come to her wedding?
Somebody had to stay home with the baby.

The Italian man had just taken a bride. When they got to the honeymoon suite, the Sicilian decided he should begin the relationship on the right note. He took off his trousers, then tossed them to his bride and said, "Put these on."

She protested. "They're way too big."

"That's right," he lectured. "I want you to know that I'm the one who wears the pants in this family."

She grimaced, but continued undressing. When she was done, she stood up, tossed her underwear to her husband, and said, "Put these on."

He looked at the dainty thing and replied, "Hey, I can't get into your pants."

"That's right," she replied. "And you never will, unless your bullshit macho attitude changes."

After the wedding, the Italian couple flew to Vegas and checked into the honeymoon suite. The next morning, the husband called room service and ordered two eggs sunny-side up, an order of sausage, a pot of coffee, and a head of lettuce. When the waiter arrived, he asked, "The eggs and sausage are for me. Give the lettuce to my wife."

"Just lettuce, sir?" the waiter asked.

"Yeah," the guy replied. "I wanna see if she eats like a rabbit, too."

Why do Italian husbands kiss their wives on the snatch before they leave for work?
Because their wives' breath stinks so bad in the morning.

Why did the Italian guy call his wife "Crisco?"
She had so much fat in the can.

The entire population of the small Italian village gathered in the center of town to see the big attraction of the traveling carnival—a donkey said to be worth 10 million lire.

One old farmer turned to a friend and said, "I don't understand how a donkey can be worth so much money."

"Because," the man replied, "if you stand real close, you can see that the donkey has a pussy just like a woman's."

The farmer started to roar with laughter. The man stared at him, then finally asked, "What's so funny?"

The farmer shook his head. "Just to think. I got a wife with a pussy like a donkey's, and she isn't worth one lire!"

The Mafia big shot walked into the furrier's store and announced, "My wife caught me with my girlfriend again, and I gotta buy a fur for her."

"Mink?" the salesman asked.

"She's got one."

"Fox?"

"She's got one."

"Sable?"

"She got one of those, too. Ain't you got anything different?"

"Well," the furrier replied, "what about skunk?"

"Skunk?" the husband asked.

"Why not? It's just a pussy that smells bad."

The mafioso said, "She's got one of those, too."

Two Italian men were walking home one day discussing their wives' spending habits. One finally turned to the other and said, "Mario, I don't understand how that woman spends so much money. She don't drink, she don't smoke, she don't gamble, and she's got her own pussy!"

Why do they put a pile of shit in the corner at an Italian wedding?
To keep the flies off the bride.

What's an Italian wife's favorite bedtime story?
"No."

What's the difference between an Italian wife and a volcano?
A volcano doesn't fake eruptions.

What's the difference between an Italian wife and poverty?
Poverty sucks.

Two Italians were brought to court for fighting. One guy defended himself by saying, "That bastard Mario made me hit him. He said my wife was the ugliest, dirtiest, smelliest, hairiest old whore in town."

The judge replied, "That's terrible. Why don't you bring your wife down to testify against him, too?"

Angelo suddenly looked uncomfortable. "Uh, your honor . . . I'd like to know one thing. Will it hurt my case if he's telling the truth?"

A man walked into an Italian restaurant and ordered a glass of vino and a piece of overripe goat cheese. The waiter's eyebrows rose in astonishment, but he complied with the request.

The man drank one glass of wine, but didn't touch the cheese. He consumed a second, then a third glass, but still left the Limburger alone. Finally, the waiter's curiosity got the best of him.

" 'Scuse me," the waiter said. "But I can't help wondering why you ordered such a stinking cheese with your wine. Then you don't touch it."

The man replied, "When I drink wine at home, my wife's sitting next to me."

What do you call an Italian woman who finds no fault with her husband?
A widow.

Carmine closed up the pizzeria early on Christmas Eve, handed the day's huge cash receipts to his daughter, loaded his wife's Christmas present, a 25-inch console color TV, into the backseat, and started home. They had a flat tire just as they were about to get on the expressway. As the man was changing it, a gang of three youths approached and robbed them.

When the young man fled, Carmine wailed, *"Mama Mia!* They tooka everything?"

"No, they didn't, Papa," his daughter said. "I stuffed the money from today up my cunt."

"Mama mia!" the Italian wailed again.

"What's wrong now, Papa?" the daughter asked.

"It's too bad your mama didn't work today," the pizza man complained. "If she'd been with us, we wouldn't have lost the TV set!"

Why is a car engine like an Italian wife?
On a cold morning, when you really need it, it won't turn over.

What's the difference between an Italian's wife and his mistress?
The difference between night and day.

What's the average Italian husband's favorite seven-course dinner?
A pizza and a six-pack.

An Italian construction worker was on his lunch hour when he succumbed to the invitation of a beautiful blond hooker standing on the corner. They retreated to a nearby hotel, where he rented a room for an hour. When he went down to check out, the desk clerk handed him a bill for nearly $3,000.

"You crazy or something?" the guinea screamed. "I wasn't even here an hour."

"You're Masucci, right?" the clerk asked.

"Yeah. But what's that gotta do with the bill?"

"Your wife's been using a room every day for two months."

The war between two Mafia families claimed another victim, and the cops dropped the body off at Santucci's Funeral Home. Santucci was laying out the hood's body when he noticed the guy had an unbelievably long penis. He called to his receptionist, "Hey, Angela. You gotta see this."

Angela came in, took a look, then said, "That's just like my husband's dick."

The mortician asked in amazement, "You mean he's got one that long?"

"No," she replied. "That dead."

Ricco came home unexpectedly and found his wife in bed with another man. Furious, he cried, "What the hell you think you're doing?"

"See," his wife said to the guy, "I told you he was stupid."

Two Italian women were talking about a friend. One said, "Angelica is so thin. I heard that she suffers from bulimia."

The other woman shook her head. "It's not bulimia, it's her husband. Every time he takes off his clothes, she throws up."

One Italian guy was talking to another at the bar and said, "My wife looks sort of like a mermaid."

"What do you mean, sort of?"

"Her top half looks like a fish."

Why is an Italian wife like a turtle?
She's slow, wrinkled, and can't get off her back.

Name three things the average Italian husband can do in three minutes?
Drain a can of beer, belch, and make love to his wife.

Why is the average Italian husband like a rodeo rider?
They only stay on for eight seconds.

Why is an Italian wife like your front door?
They both have mail slots.

An Italian woman was laying in bed late one night, unable to sleep. Finally, she poked her husband awake and said, "Frank, I've gotta know. If I died, would you marry again?"

"I suppose so," he replied.

"Would you sleep with her in this bed?" the wife asked.

"It's the only bed in the house," the husband replied.

"Would you make love to her?"

"Honey," the husband said, "of course. We'd be married. Now, go to sleep."

"One more question," she said. "Would you let her drive my car?"

"No," the husband replied. "She doesn't know how to drive a stick shift."

What's an Italian marriage?
A ceremony that turns your dreamboat into a barge.

What's a classy Italian wedding reception?
The organ grinder brings two monkeys.

Marcotti's wife died, and the priest was conducting the last rites at the gravesite. The man was hysterical, weeping and tearing at his hair. After the casket was lowered, the priest came over to the man, who was moaning, "Whata my gonna do? Whata my gonna do?"

The father put his arm around Marcotti and said, "There, there, my son. I know you loved your wife. But this grief will pass."

The man ignored him, moaning, "Whata my gonna do?"

The priest continued, "Your anguish is fresh now. But in a year, or two, or three, you'll meet another woman, fall in love, and get married."

The man looked up at him and said, "Father, I know that. But whata my gonna do tonight?"

Parlucci went to the doctor and told him that something had to be done. "My wife just hadda kid number ten. We don't want no more."

The doctor reached into a drawer, pulled out a small package, and said, "This is a condom. Right before you have sex, stretch it out over your organ."

Parlucci nodded and went home. A month later, he barged into the doctor's office and announced, "My wife, she's gonna have another kid. That thing you gave me didn't work."

The doctor asked, "Didn't you stretch it out over your organ."

"We ain't got an organ. I stretched it over the piano."

Angelo went to see a lawyer about a divorce. The attorney asked, "What grounds do you have?"

Angelo replied, "I gotta da front yard, da backyard, and a little strip onna side."

"I meant," the lawyer continued, "do you have a grudge?"

"Yeah," Angelo replied. "But it's so fulla stuff, we can't get the car in."

Frustrated, the lawyer asked, "Is your wife a nagger?"

"Nah," the Italian replied. "But I caught her screwing one. That's why I wanna divorce."

Vito came home unexpectedly one day to find his wife screwing a naked man in his bed. He pulled out a shotgun and was about to fire when his wife said, "Vito, wait. Who do you think bought us the mink coat, the new twenty-five-inch TV, and the new Cadillac?"

"Are you the man?" Vito asked.

The guy nodded.

Vito reached into the closet and pulled out a blanket. "Here," he said to the guy. "Cover yourself. We don't want you catching cold while you're fucking."

John Voccoti got into the habit of staying out very late every night. His wife nagged him unmercifully for a while. Then, for a few nights, she remained totally silent while he slipped into bed.

Nervous, Voccoti came home one night, slipped beneath the sheets, then said, "Good night, mother of four."

His wife replied, "Good night, father of one."

Voccoti was home by five the next day.

What's a happily married Italian couple?
A guy who's out with another man's wife.

CHAPTER 4

GREAT JOKES ABOUT RELIGION

Why wasn't Christ born in Italy?
They couldn't find three wise men and a virgin.

A drunken old Italian man reeking of cheap wine, cigars, and perfume, staggered up the stairs of the bus, reeled down the aisle, then plopped down in the seat next to Father Martelli.

The drunk took a long look at his shocked seat partner, then said, "Padre. I gotta question for you. What causes arthritis?"

The priest replied in a cold, curt voice, "Amoral living. Too much wine, smoking, and consorting with prostitutes."

"Huh," the drunk replied. "Well, I'll be damned."

They rode in silence for a moment. The priest began to feel guilty that he'd reacted so strongly to a man who obviously needed Christian compassion. He turned to his seat partner and said, "I am sorry. I didn't mean to be harsh. How long have you suffered from the affliction of arthritis?"

"Me?" the drunk replied. "I don't have arthritis. I read in the paper that the Pope's got it."

The Pope was having increasingly frequent attacks of chest pains that were preventing him from carrying out his holy tasks. The College of Cardinals finally called in the world's leading cardiologist from New York, who examined the Pontiff for hours.

Finally, he said to the Pope, "Your heart is fine. It's stress that's killing you. It's been building up all of your life, and there's only one way to get rid of it—you've got to have sex with a woman."

The Pontiff argued with the doctor, but in the end was convinced of the validity of his diagnosis. For days, a debate raged among the cardinals until a consensus was reached that if sex could save the Pope's life, it must be God's will.

The Pope yielded to his cardinals. But he insisted on three conditions that the woman must meet. "First, she must be blind, so she cannot see where she is being taken. Two, she must be deaf and dumb, so she can never speak of what she experienced."

"Yes, Your Holiness," the cardinals replied. "And what's your third conditions?"

"She's gotta have big, big tits."

There was bad flooding in Venice one spring and the water rose over the banks of the canals and began flooding the buildings. An evacuation was ordered for the entire city, and boats began picking up residents to ferry them to the mainland. When the rescue boat came up beside one four-story building, a devoutly Catholic old Italian woman refused to leave her second-story apartment. The boatsman pleaded with her, but the woman replied, "The Lord will provide."

The water continued to rise. A little later, an Italian navy cutter came by the building and spotted the old woman on the third floor. They shouted at her to come aboard, but the old woman said, "The Lord will provide."

The water rose more in the nearly empty city. An hour later, a lone gondolier steered his boat by the building. He saw the woman stranded on the top floor and steered over to rescue her. Once again she said, "The Lord will provide."

Shortly afterward, the water rose, drowning the old woman. She soon arrived at the Pearly Gates, where she angrily demanded to see Jesus. Ushered into the presence of the Son of God, she shouted, "All my life, I light candles every day and pray to the Virgin, Your mama. But when I need Your help, You abandon me."

"Abandon you?" Jesus replied. "What more could I do? I sent three boats."

A young nun rushed into the mother superior's office and exclaimed, "We've just discovered a case of syphilis in the convent!"

"Thank the Lord!" the mother superior replied. "I'm sick to death of Chianti."

The nuns ran an orphanage for young girls in a remote corner of Sicily in order to remove them from the temptations of the world. One day, it was time for three teenage girls to leave the orphanage. Mother Superior called them in and announced, "You've spent your lives far away from that sinful world which you now must confront. I must warn you that men will try to take advantage of you. They will buy you flowers, then wine and food. After you are intoxicated, they will take you back to their apartments, remove your clothes, and do indecent things to your bodies. Then they will give you a few hundred lire and cast you out."

The girls looked shocked. One finally asked, "You mean men will take advantage of us and actually give us money?"

"Yes, child," Mother Superior replied. "Does that surprise you?"

"It certainly does," the girl replied. "The priests only give us candy."

A sociologist flew to Italy as part of a survey of the sexual habits of various European nations. He drove to a small village near Naples, walked into a café, and spotted an old man dressed in black sipping wine at a table in the corner. He approached and asked the man if he'd mind answering a few questions about his sex life. The man shrugged, indicating his willingness.

The sociologist pressed the record button on his tape recorder, then asked, "How many times a year do you have sexual intercourse?"

The man replied, "Maybe five, maybe six."

The sociologist was shocked. "I'm amazed. Italian men are supposed to be so virile."

"Now wait a minute," the offended man replied. "Five or six times a year, it's not so bad for an old priest in a tiny village."

Father Rinaldi paid a visit one morning to one of the women in his parish. When he was ushered into the living room, he was surprised to see a sheet with a round hole in the middle hanging across the doorway leading to the kitchen. The priest asked what the sheet was for. The woman hesitated for a moment, then said, "Father, a big group from the parish was here last night drinking wine. One thing led to another, and the men ended up taking turns sticking their dicks through the hole so we could try to guess who they were."

"That's outrageous!" the man of God exclaimed. "If I had been here, I would have been shocked."

"I'm sure you would have been," the woman replied. "Your name was guessed six times."

How did the Italian priest make holy water?
Put some regular water in a pot and boiled the hell out of it.

Why did the Italian kid rape the nun?
He just got into the habit.

Little Giuseppe learned to pray. The first night he ended his prayers with, "God bless Grandpa." The very next morning, his grandfather dropped dead at the breakfast table. The little boy tried to tell his parents what happened, but they were too upset to listen.

The next night, Giuseppe ended his prayers with "God bless Grandma." Sure enough, they found Grandma's body the next day. By this time, his family was listening, and they sternly warned Giuseppe not to mention any names in his prayers. For several days, he followed the instructions. But finally, he forgot, ending his prayer with "God bless Papa."

His father turned white. After a sleepless night, the haunted man left the house after breakfast and went straight to the church. As he knelt in the pew, he suddenly went stiff with shock. The priest was lying dead on the altar.

Sister Maria and Sister Angela were walking into town when a man leaped out of the bushes. He pulled one nun to the ground and raped her.

When it was over, Sister Maria asked the other nun, "What are we going to do? How can I explain to the police I was raped twice in one night?"

"Twice?" the puzzled Sister Angela asked.

"Well, we are coming back this way, aren't we?"

What's black and white and black and white and black and white and black and white and black and white and black and white and black and white and black and white and black and white? A nun an Italian kid pushed down the stairs.

How could Monsignor Calvi tell that the nun was really horny? She had a vibrating crucifix.

Why are there so few Italian monks? The vow of silence includes farting.

Did you hear about the Sicilian priest who presided over so many shotgun weddings? He named his church Winchester Cathedral.

Why did the Pope flash the Sistine Chapel?
He wanted to expose himself to art.

Father Masucci had seen the attendance at Sunday Mass dwindle over the course of months. He went to Palermo to see the bishop, who told him to lighten up his sermons. The good father pondered this during the train ride back to his village. Then, the next Sunday, he told his parishioners, "We are going to depart from the scripture today to ask a few questions. Tell me, how many of you have seen a ghost?"

At least half the congregation raised their hands.

"That's interesting," Father Masucci said. "Now, how many of you have actually talked to a ghost?"

The number of hands dwindled to about a dozen. The priest said, "One last question. How many of you have had sexual relations with a ghost?"

At first, no one moved. Then Vito Cavelli slowly put his hand into the air. Father Masucci glared at him. "Vito, stand up."

The man complied.

The priest questioned, "Do you mean to tell us that you actually had sex with a ghost?"

The man's worried look vanished. "No, Father," Vito replied. "I thought you said 'goat.' "

What's black and white and black and white and black and white and black and white?
A priest and nun screwing.

Father Calvi was walking through the church one day when he noticed something. He went over, nodded at a bulge in a nun's habit, and said, "Sister Maria, aren't you putting on some weight?"

Sister Maria replied, nervously, "Oh, Father, it's just a little gas."

A couple months later Father Calvi was visiting a sick nun in the convent when he noticed that Sister Maria's habit was stretched out tight. He made another remark, and the nun replied, "Oh, it's just a little gas."

A month later, Father Calvi emerged from the church to see Sister Maria pushing a baby carriage. He peeked in and said, "So that's the little fart."

Angelo walked into the confessional, knelt down, then said, "Bless me, Father, for I have sinned."

"How have you sinned, my son?" the priest asked.

"Father, when I am in bed making love to my

wife, I often dream about screwing one of the nuns."

"God will forgive you," the priest replied. "When I'm in bed with one of the nuns, I often dream about screwing your wife."

Sixteen-year-old Maria came to the church one night and asked for a special meeting with Father Margoni. She shyly admitted that a boy had taken advantage of her, but she blushed when the father asked her to describe what happened.

"Did he do this?" the priest asked, kissing her.

"Yes, and worse," the girl replied.

The priest ran his hands over the girl's voluptuous breasts and asked, "Did he do this?"

"Yes, and worse."

The priest was now breathing heavily. He thrust his hand inside her skirt and fingered her. "Did he do this?"

"Yes, and worse."

Father Margoni could no longer restrain himself. He tore off the girl's clothes, laid her down on a pew, and proceeded to enter her. As he pumped away, he panted, "Did he do this?"

"Yes," said Maria, "and worse."

"What could be worse?" the priest panted.

"He gave me the clap, Father."

CHAPTER 5

GREAT JOKES ABOUT ITALIAN WOMEN

An American woman, a French woman, and an Italian woman were in the lingerie department buying panties. The salesclerk turned to the American woman and asked how many pairs she'd need.

"Seven," the American woman replied. "One pair for each day of the week."

Next came the French girl, who said she'd need five pairs. "One for each day Monday through Friday. On the weekends, I am with my lover and I don't wear panties."

The salesclerk wrote the order down, then turned to the Italian woman to ask how many pairs she'd need.

"Twelve," the Italian woman replied. "January, February, March . . ."

Why did the Italian man have his wife douche with Crest?
He'd heard it reduced cavities.

Why did the Italian guy trade his wife for an outhouse?
The hole was smaller and it smelled better.

How can you tell a pregnant Italian woman's going to have a son?
If she's happy. Italian women are always happy with a prick in them.

The Italian girl walked into the store in her small town and told the proprietor that she was in love with an American GI. "One thing," she said, "he's a little weird about." She lifted up her arm and pointed to the growth underneath. "He wants me to get ridda this. You got something?"

The proprietor nodded. A few minutes later she walked out of the store with hedge clippers.

After nine children, the Italian woman went to the doctor and said, "Enough is enough. I don't want to have any more kids."

The doctor gave her some birth-control pills. Four months later, she walked into his office, obviously pregnant. "What happened?" he asked. "Did you take a pill every day?"

"I did," she replied. "But they kept falling out."

What's the difference between Italian starlets and French starlets?
French starlets don't have mustaches.

How do Italian parents know their daughter is old enough to date?
They make her stand up and hold her arms straight out to the side. If her armpit hair touches the floor, she's old enough.

How can you tell if a woman is half-Irish and half-Italian?
She mashes potatoes with her feet.

Why do Italian girls wear sleeveless dresses?
They love the feeling of wind blowing through their hair.

At the Miss Universe contest, how do you identify Miss Italy?
She's the one who looks like she has a Brillo pad under each armpit.

Why did the Italian woman limp?
She cut her toes shaving.

Did you hear about the Italian woman who was pondering a new hairdo?
She couldn't decide whether to have the hair on her legs braided or curled.

What do "The NFL Today" and the Miss Italy Contest have in common?
They're both pigskin previews.

Why do Italian men grow mustaches?
So they can look like their mothers.

What's the difference between an Italian grandmother and a hippo?
A hippo can't make spaghetti sauce.

How can you tell if an Italian woman is having her period?
She's only wearing one sock.

How can you tell if an Italian woman is wearing panty hose?
Her ankles swell up when she farts.

What's a fuck-off?
A tiebreaker at the Miss Italy contest.

What's the first thing an Italian wife does before she takes a bath?
Greases the sides of the tub so she won't get stuck.

An Italian girl fell in love with a classical musician, but her mother was violently opposed to the match.

"What's wrong?" the musician asked. "I make a good living."

"It's not that," the girl replied, "It's . . . well, my mother thinks you're too feminine."

"She may have a point," the musician replied. "Her mustache is certainly a lot thicker than mine."

What do you call a voluptuous Italian woman?
A pizza ass.

How do Italian women protect themselves from Peeping Toms?
They keep the curtains open.

How did the Italian woman take off twenty pounds in one day?
She washed off her makeup.

Why don't Italian women shave their legs?
They put them up in curlers.

Why did the Italian man return the fur coat he bought for his wife?
The fur clashed with her mustache.

What's the most effective form of birth control for an Italian woman?
Her face.

Why did God create Sicilian woman?
Because sheep can't cook spaghetti.

After his parents died, Luigi decided to travel to Italy to see the rural village in which they'd been born. Arriving in the country, he accepted an invitation to stay with his cousin. The first thing he did after he settled in was to borrow a shotgun to go hunting, because his father had told him so many stories about hunting as a boy. Luigi walked down a country road, then across a field. Suddenly, an animal appeared and Luigi fired. Unaware that his victim was a goat, Luigi ran back to his cousin's house and announced, "I shot something."

"Describe it to me," his cousin said.

"Well, it had two tits, a scruffy beard, and a stinking ass."

"Oh, no!" the cousin exclaimed. "You've shot my wife!"

The nun noticed Angela walking into school with a scarf hiding her face. She went up to the girl and demanded, "What's wrong?"

Angela replied, "Sister, I'm ashamed. I gotta black eye."

The nun shook her head. "How many times do I have to tell you? Don't jump rope without a bra on."

Why did the Italian hooker try to stab the madam? She'd been working in the whorehouse for five years—then she discovered the other girls got paid.

Why don't Italian girls shave their legs?
Fur leggings are in this year.

What do grapes do when an Italian woman stomps on them?
Let out a little wine.

A guy was out on a date with an Italian girl, and the going got hot and heavy. The guy worked his hand into her pants, and she was moaning with pleasure when suddenly she grunted in pain. "Hey," she complained, "take that ring off. It's hurting me."

The guy replied, "That's no ring—it's my wristwatch."

Why are all Italian women whores?
They don't give a fuck for nothing.

What happens when an Italian girl invites some men to her party?
Everybody comes.

How can you find out which Italian girl gives the best blow jobs?
Word of mouth.

What's an Italian "10"?
No mustache.

How can you tell an Italian woman's fat?
Her LaCoste shirt has a hippo on it.

What's the sexiest four-letter word to an Italian woman?
Cash.

What's so embarrassing about being introduced to an Italian mother-in-law?
One look and you don't know whether to shake her hand or sniff her ass.

How do we know that Italian girls aren't made out of sugar and spice?
They taste like anchovies.

Why do so many teenage Italian girls get pregnant?
Their mothers never teach them to give a decent blow job.

Why are a lot of Italian girls like prizefighters?
They won't go into action until they see a ring.

What's hairy, wrinkled, and hangs out underwear?
An Italian mother-in-law.

Why don't Italian women have hair on their chests?
Did you ever see grass growing on a playground?

Why is an Italian woman like a toilet seat?
Without a hole in the middle, she wouldn't be good for shit.

How can you tell if an Italian girl has a huge cunt?
Her gynecologist is a member of the United Mine Workers.

Why did the old Italian woman suddenly look twenty years younger?
Her tits finally sagged so much they took the wrinkles out of her face.

Why do Italian women have cunts?
So men will talk to them.

Why did the birth rate in Italy go up dramatically?
The supermarkets got in a fresh shipment of paper bags.

Why do fisherman like to marry Italian women?
Italian women usually have a fine crop of worms.

An Italian girl saw a girlfriend in a store buying a false beard. "What are you doing with that?" she asked as her friend tried the beard on.

"Can't you tell?" the friend asked. "I've been invited to a cocktail party, and I'm going as my armpit."

Why is a dresser like an Italian woman?
Neither ever changes their drawers.

What do football players and Italian girls have in common?
They both shower after the fourth period.

Why do Italian women wear such high-heeled shoes?
To keep their tits from dragging on the ground.

How can you tell if an Italian woman is really fat?
She doesn't have to put the toilet seat down when
she pees.

Why is an Italian girl like a carriage horse?
They both have a buggy behind.

Why is an Italian girl like a politician?
They both say yes to every proposition.

Why did the dentist charge double for the Italian
woman?
She had the biggest cavity he ever drilled.

What's the difference between an Italian girl and
garbage?
Garbage gets picked up.

The Italian spinster went to the doctor and admitted that she'd tried to pay men to have sex with her. But all of them fled, complaining that her cunt stank. She couldn't see how that could be true, because when she bent over, she couldn't smell a thing.

The doctor examined her, then said, "You need an operation."

"On my pussy?" she asked.

"On your nose," the doctor replied.

Why did God invent wine?
So Italian women would have a chance to get laid.

Did you hear about the old Italian countess who had her face lifted eleven times?
If she has it done once more, she'll be a bearded lady.

Why don't Italian women wear yellow?
So people don't yell "Taxi!" at them.

Why are an Italian woman's tits like a sweet chariot?
They both swing low.

How can you tell an Italian woman in a cow pasture?
She's the one without the bell.

It was the guy's first day at the sex aids store. His very first customer was a white woman, who asked about the price of dildos. The man replied, "Well, I've got this sleek white Warren Beatty model for $39.95 and this big black Mike Tyson model for $49.95." The girl buys the black dildo and leaves.

The second customer was a black chick, also looking for a self-amusement rod. The salesman offers her the same models, but switches the price. Sure enough, the black girl goes for the white model.

Proud of himself, he moved on to his third customer, an Italian girl who also asked to see dildos. The salesman said, "I've got this white one at $39.95, this black one at $49.95, and this red one at $79.95." The Italian girl took the red one, paid, and left the store.

A couple minutes later, the store owner walked in and asked the salesman, "How's business?"

"Pretty good," the guy said, "I sold a white one, a black one, and the fire extinguisher."

How do you know an Italian girl is fat?
She sprays oil and vinegar on the lawn, then grazes.

Why are there nude pictures of Italian women?
So gorillas can masturbate.

Did you hear about the special LaCoste shirts for Italian girls?
It's got a little pig on the front.

What's the difference between a WASP wedding and Italian wedding?
Before a WASP wedding, they give the bride a shower; before an Italian wedding, they make the bride take one.

Why did the people at work call the Italian girl the "office monkey."
She was hired because of her tail.

What's the four-letter word an Italian woman most frequently screams out during sex?
"NEXT!"

CHAPTER 6

GREAT JOKES ABOUT ITALIAN MEN

What can you do for an Italian with bad breath?
Pour Lavoris in the toilet.

A man went to see his physician and said, "Doc, you have to help me. I'm in love with this Polish girl. She won't marry me unless I become a Polack."

The doctor replied, "There's only one way to do that. I'll have to operate and remove half your brain."

The man was so much in love that he agreed. He checked into the hospital and a few hours later, he went under the knife.

The next morning, he came to. The doctor leaned over and said, "I'm afraid I have some very bad news. We made a mistake and removed three-quarters of your brain."

The man cried, *"Mama mia!"*

What do you get when you cross an Italian and a gorilla?
A moron who doesn't need winter underwear.

An Italian was sitting at the bar having a few drinks when the news came on. The first story showed a man standing on the ledge of a tall building, threatening to jump. The bartender said to the Italian, "Ten bucks says he jumps."

The Italian took the bet. Sure enough, the guy jumped. The Italian reached into his pocket, pulled out a wad of small bills and change, and slowly counted out ten dollars.

The bartender watched him, then said, "Listen, I have a confession to make. I saw this story on the early news. I knew the guy was going to jump, so you keep the ten bucks."

"No, you keep it," the Italian said. "I saw the early news, too. I didn't think the guy'd be so dumb he'd jump again."

What's foreplay for an Italian man?
Whistling.

What's a formal Italian dinner?
One where all the men come to the table with their flies zipped.

Why do Italian men like women with big tits and small pussies?
Because Italian men have big mouths and small dicks.

What's an Italian man's idea of oral sex?
Shouting "Fuck you!" at a woman walking down the street.

Did you hear about the lazy Italian?
He married a pregnant woman.

Why do Italian men have such big noses?
They're handpicked.

A housewife was passing the cart of an Italian fruit peddler when the man called out, "Please, lady, take a look at my melons."

She stopped, came over, picked up a cantaloupe, took a sniff, then announced, "I can't buy this. It stinks."

The Italian got a big smile. "No, it's not the melon. It'sa me that stinks."

Why is it that only Italian women get hemorrhoids? When God created Italian men, he created the perfect asshole.

Why do Italian men talk with their hands? Their breath will kill you.

Why did the Italian invent the new drug that's part aphrodisiac and part laxative? His motto was, "Easy come, easy go."

What does every Italian man have that gets bigger when you stroke it? His ego.

Why was Paul Revere like an Italian in a whore-house?
They're both minute men.

What did the Italian guy do when his girlfriend asked him to do something kinky?
Peed in her sink.

Why don't Italians wear short-sleeved shirts?
Ever wipe your nose on your bare arm?

What does an Italian have that's six inches long and proves he's a man?
His birth certificate.

Why are so many Italian men called Tony?
Because when the boat got to Ellis Island, some-one stamped "TO N.Y." on their foreheads.

Why are Italian men like public toilets?
They're either taken or full of shit.

Little Maria watched her papa take a shower.
She noticed his testicles and asked him about them.
"Those are my tomatoes," he replied.

Quickly, the little girl ran into the kitchen and
told her mother what Papa had said. Her mother
grimaced and asked, "Did Papa tell you about the
dead branch they were hanging on?"

What does the perfect Italian male look like?
Long, dark, and handsome.

What's the definition of frenzy?
An Italian with a credit card in a whorehouse.

A Italian guy was walking in the neighborhood
when he saw a beautiful girl walking her dog. He

slowed down as he approached her, then winked. To his surprise, the dog got a huge hard-on.

He walked past, circled the block, then headed back toward the girl. He stopped next to her and was about to ask her for a date when the dog got a hard-on again.

"What's wrong with the dog?" he asked the girl.

"Nothing's wrong with him," the girl said.

"Why did he get a hard-on twice?"

"Simple," the girl said. "He knows that Italian guys like you are all cocksuckers."

An Italian stud complained to a woman at a singles bar, "I can't find a decent woman. No one I meet is fit for a pig to screw."

She looked at him icily, then replied, "If you keep talking like that, I'm sure you'll meet one who is."

The cocktail-lounge Romeo slid his hand up the young lady's thigh and crooned, "How about us going back to your place so I can slip you eight inches?"

"No way," she replied. "I don't really think you can get it up four times in a row."

The Italian dude tried everything he could think of to get the beautiful girl at the end of the bar to notice him. Finally, angered by his lack of success, he walked up to her, stared for a moment, then said sarcastically, "Sorry. For a minute, I thought you were my mother."

"I couldn't be," she replied coolly. "I'm married."

How do you circumcise an Italian?
Wop.

What do you get if you cross a retarded Puerto Rican with a baboon?
An Italian intellectual.

Why don't Italian men ever make love to their wives in the morning?
You never know who you're gonna meet in the afternoon.

Did you hear about the Italian guy who died cooking dinner?
He put his nose in the microwave.

Why don't Italian dogs do any tricks?
To teach a dog tricks, the owner has to be smarter than the dog.

Why is an Italian man like a mailman?
You never know when he's going to come, and when he does, half the time it's in someone else's box.

CHAPTER 7

GREAT JOKES ABOUT ITALIANS AND CRIME

Why did the mafioso buy $5,000 worth of Cadillac tires?
He wanted his living room to have white walls.

How does the newspaper report of an Italian social event read?
"Among those wounded by gunshots were . . ."

How many Italians does it take to change a light bulb?
Four. One to steal it, one to do it, one to watch, and one to shoot the witness.

What do eating pussy and the Mafia have in common?
One slip of the tongue and you're in deep shit.

Did you hear about the Italian who was asked to become a Jehovah's Witness?
He refused because he didn't see the shooting.

What do the godfather and a two-inch cock have in common?
No one wants to fuck with either one of them.

What do you get when you cross a male porno star with a loan shark?
Someone who's always into you for at least twelve inches.

Why was the mafioso so violently opposed to his daughter marrying a black dude?
He didn't want his grandchildren to be too lazy to steal.

How can you tell if a Polack is at a cockfight?
He enters a duck.
How can you tell if an Irishman is at a cockfight?
He bets on the duck.
How can you tell if an Italian is at a cockfight?
The duck wins.

The godfather of the Mafia family made so much money that he decided to go legit. He hired the best London tailors, traded in his flashy cars for a Rolls-Royce, enrolled his sons in prep school, joined a snobbish country club, then bought a bank and named himself president. His only worry was that his chorus-girl-mistress Bambi would embarrass him with his new high-society friends.

He pondered the problem, then his lawyer suggested that he ship Bambi off to England to a fancy finishing school. He followed that advice. For three months, he received glowing weekly reports of her progress.

Finally, she arrived back in the States. She walked into his office and asked, "Darling, were you blue while I was gone?"

"Christ almighty!" the don exclaimed. "Ten grand in tuition, and you ain't even got your tenses right."

Why did the Mafia gangster's girlfriend walk out on him?
She found out he was just a finger man.

Rocco walked into the mob hangout with a shiny black eye. "What's the matter?" his friend asked.
"That bitch, Maria. I called her a two-bit whore."
"What'd she hit you with?"
"A bag of quarters."

How can you tell if a Mafia guy has several mistresses?
His wife's got it pretty soft.

What's the difference between baseball and the Mafia?
In baseball, if you're caught stealing, you're out.

Why did the Mafia guy start screwing the wife of a friend who was sent to the slammer?
He had it in for him.

The mob lawyer got a call in the middle of the night and went down to central booking to find one of the wise guys who was locked up in the slammer. He asked, "What did they get you for, loan sharking?"

"Nothing like that," the mobster replied. "I shot my wife. She called me a lousy lover."

The lawyer looked at him with astonishment. "You murdered your wife for calling you names?"

"Nah," the gangster replied. "I shot her for knowing the difference."

How does a Mafia soldier bring love into the world?
He spends his day fucking people.

Why do members of the Mafia attract so many beautiful women?
They're crack shots.

Why are Mafia hoods so smart?
They come up with a concrete solution to every problem.

When does a Mafia button man become a respectable businessman?
When he marries your daughter.

The new Mafia don finally got married, and he took his wife to Atlantic City for their honeymoon. His wife was impressed when everyone, from the valet parking attendant to the concierge to the desk clerk greeted the godfather by name while scraping and bowing. She stroked his arm lovingly while they waited for the elevator to take them to the honeymoon suite.

The doors opened. Standing inside was an incredibly well-built blonde in a tiny bikini. She took one look, then said, "Well, Johnny D. How have you been?"

He mumbled, "Okay." Then they rode in icy silence until she departed at the seventh floor. The don's bride turned to him and demanded, "Who was that bimbo?"

"Get off my back," the godfather replied. "I'm gonna have a tough enough time explaining you to her."

Did you hear about the mobster whose blond bombshell kept demanding expensive gifts?
A year later, he had to marry her for his money.

What's another name for screwing a Mafia guy?
Racket balling.

What happened when the car backfired outside an Italian restaurant?
Half the customers shot the other half.

Why did the Mafia guy put soap in the K-Y jelly?
He wanted his girlfriend to come clean.

Why did the police department stop assigning female detectives to tail mobsters?
They kept blowing their assignments.

What's the worst thing for a mobster's wife to say when her husband wants to fuck her?
"Over my dead body."

What should you say to a Sicilian guy in a three-piece suit?
"Will the defendant please rise. . . ."

The young mobster was on his daily rounds, collecting money from the numbers runners in the ghetto, when he heard moans from the alley. He investigated. Behind a bunch of trash cans he saw a beautiful young woman, completely naked, tied to the ground by four stakes. He went over to her and asked, "What happened to you?"

"Thank God you found me," she panted. "I got off the subway at the wrong stop. The minute I came up onto the street, eight guys surrounded me. They dragged me into the alley, tied me up like this, raped me, then ran off with all my money and jewelry."

The hoodlum shook his head for a moment as he stared at her. Then he started unbuckling his gun belt, saying, "Well, lady, it looks like today just ain't going to be your day."

What do you find under the hood of an Italian car?
His girlfriend.

Why is screwing the Mafia like screwing a fat girl?
You have a good chance of being bumped off.

What does a mobster do if a guy tries to steal his wife?
He lets him.

Why didn't the mobster know the name of the girl he screwed last night?
His philosophy was shoot first, ask questions later.

The Mafia don turned to his mistress in bed just after sex and asked, "Hey, babe, what would you do if you found you were knocked up?"

"Oh, that's horrible," the pretty girl exclaimed. "I'm sure I'd kill myself."

The godfather patted her on the head. "Good girl."

After the Mafia family's annual Christmas party, one wise guy woke up with a gigantic hangover. He turned over and asked his wife, "What in the hell happened last night?"

"As usual," the wife replied, "you made a total ass of yourself in front of the don."

"Piss on him," the husband said.

"You did. Then he put out a contract on you."

"Fuck him," the mobster growled.

"I did," the wife replied. "You go back to working the same numbers operation on Monday."

The family of an eighteen-year-old Sicilian girl gave her in marriage to the eighty-one-year-old godfather of the local Mafia family. A few weeks later, the bride ran into a friend of hers in church, and the friend asked, "How is married life with Don Carlissimo?"

The teenager grimaced. "Oh," she said, "it's the same old thing, weak in, weak out."

Did you hear about the guy who ran into a Mafia bar and yelled *"fire"*?
Everyone did.

The girl turned to the Mafia guy who was in bed with her and asked, "Can you fuck me and hurt me?"

"Sure," he replied. Then he fucked her and hit her over the head with a brick.

Why did the young Italian hoodlum deliberately get himself locked up in jail?
To keep his face from breaking out.

How do you know there's an organized-crime war going on in your town?
The funeral home runs a Valentine's Day sale.

The godfather lay in the oxygen tent, with his oldest son at his side. Hours previously, he had told his heir that he would inherit leadership of the family, along with all the revenue from gambling, loan sharking, bootlegging, racketeering, prostitution, and drugs.

The weeping son whispered, his voice choked with emotion, "Godfather, Godfather, I am so grateful. But I still feel unworthy. Is there anything I can do for you . . . anything?"

"Well, son," the godfather gasped, "I'd appreciate it very much if you took your foot off the oxygen hose."

After sex, the young bride cuddled up to her husband, a rising star in the Mafia. She said, "Darling, something seems to be bothering you. Is it me?"

He squeezed her reassuringly and said, "No, babe. It don't got nothing to do with you."

She insisted on knowing what was wrong. Finally, he said, "If you really want to know, I'm pissed off. When I dropped my girlfriend off at the maternity ward last night, she had the nerve to say that I didn't care about her."

Did you hear about the dumbest Mafia guy? When a guy double-crossed him, he put his feet in cement and tossed him into a wading pool.

What do you get when you cross an Italian with a Pole?
A hit man who misses.

At an Italian wedding, how can you tell the difference between the Mafia guys and the musicians?
The musicians are the ones without the violin cases.

Did you hear about the strange new Italian car called the Mafia?
The hood is in the front seat and the body's in the trunk.

Did you hear about the Italian who knew the exact day, hour, and minute he was going to die?
The warden told him.

Always conscious of security, the Mafia don employed a deaf and dumb accountant to handle the money from his many illicit operations. For years, he'd been satisfied with the man's work. However, during a routine examination of the books this year, he discovered that over a million dollars was missing. Furious, he had his goons go to the guy's house and yank the accountant out of bed. In order to question the deaf and dumb man, he ordered his men to bring in the accountant's brother to translate the sign language.

When the men were in his office, the mobster demanded, "I know you've been stealing. I want to know where my money is?"

After a brief flurry of hand movement, the translator said, "My brother says he doesn't know what you're talking about."

The boss gestured to one of his goons. The hoodlum walked over to the closet, pulled out a shotgun, cocked both barrels, and held the gun to the accountant's head. The mob boss said, "Now, you little bastard. Tell me where my money is or your brains are going to be splattered all over the wall."

The brother's hands moved. The terrified accountant signed back, "Tell him I took the money. It's all in shoe boxes hidden in the back of my closet in my apartment."

The boss said to the brother, "What did he say?"

The brother replied, "He says you haven't got the balls to kill him."

The three Italian gangsters were speeding away from a stickup when the driver heard sirens. He called out over his shoulder, "Hey, Vito. See any flashing lights behind us?"

"Yeah . . . no . . . yeah . . . no . . . yeah . . . no . . ."

CHAPTER 8

GREAT JOKES ABOUT
ITALIAN CHILDREN

The eight-year-old Italian boy was hauled into court on charges of making a teenage girl pregnant. In court, his mother pleaded with the judge that her son couldn't possibly have done it. She unzipped the boy's fly, exposing his penis. "Looka, your honor," she said. "Take a look atta dat organ. It's so tiny. No way he could have—"

"Mama, please!" the boy whispered urgently. "If you donna stop stroking it, we're gonna lose this case!"

A seven-year-old Italian boy came into the house one day and said, "Mama, Rosa and me are gonna get married."

His mother, amused said, "Tony, how you gonna earn money if you get married?"

"Rosa's papa owns the pizza joint. He's got plenty of money."

Still teasing him, his mama said, "When a boy and girl get married, they have bambinos. Then what will you do?"

Tony shrugged. "So far, we been lucky."

Six-year-old Vinnie and his little friend Tony were hiding in his big sister's closet when Maria brought her boyfriend into the bedroom. Although they were only able to get glimpses of what was going on, they heard plenty of panting and moaning and groaning. Then the bed began to shake and Maria sighed, "Oh, John, you're in where no man has ever been before!"

"Gosh," Vinnie said to Tony, "he must be fucking her in the ass!"

Why do Italian children wear shoes?
To break them of the habit of biting their nails.

What are the five most difficult years for an Italian child?
The second grade.

An altar boy walked into the liquor store and told the proprietor he needed a bottle of wine.

"Get out of here," the owner said. "You're too young."

"But I need the wine for Father Petracelli." He leaned over the counter and whispered, "It's for his constipation."

The liquor-store owner pondered a moment, then handed the boy the wine. "Get off to the rectory with you."

A couple hours later, the owner locked up his shop and started for home. Half a block down the street, he was startled to see the altar boy sitting in the alley, singing at the top of his lungs and obviously drunk.

Angrily, the liquor-store owner marched up to the boy and said, "You lied to me. You said that wine was for Father Petracelli's constipation."

"It is," the lad hiccuped. "When he finds out about this, he'll shit."

Did you hear about the ugly Italian baby?
For six months, they diapered the wrong end.

The Italian family had gathered for the grandparent's fiftieth wedding anniversary. The wine flowed and the table was piled high with lasagne, manicotti, and other pasta dishes. Unfortunately, the party was being spoiled by eight-year-old Angelo, who ran through the apartment knocking glasses out of people's hands, smearing sauce-stained hands on clothes, and generally misbehaving. His indulgent mother threw up her hands at the boy's behavior. Finally, Uncle Joey got out of his chair and said, "I'll have a talk with the boy."

Uncle Joey took the boy into another room, then returned ten minutes later. First an hour, then another passed, and not a word was heard from Angelo. His mother came over and said to Joey, "You're a miracle worker. In the name of the Blessed Virgin, what did you threaten him with to keep him quiet?"

Joey shrugged. "It was nothing. I didn't threaten him. I just taught him how to masturbate."

Did you hear about the young Italian punks who went to a drive-in movie?
They didn't like the picture, so they slashed their seats.

Why do Italian mothers have such strong arms and big shoulders?
From raising dumbbells.

What do Italian mothers do when their children misbehave?
Wop 'em.

How did the Italian mother react when her daughter was born with a mustache?
She was tickled.

Why is an Italian mother like a dairy?
They both have milk in gallon jugs.

Why was the little Italian kid so upset when the label fell off his yellow crayon?
He wanted to know what color it was.

A middle-aged lady was walking down the streets of Little Italy about lunchtime when she saw a very young kid lounging against a wall while he took deep drags from his cigarette and chugged a quart bottle of beer. Outraged, she marched up to him and demanded, "Young man, why aren't you in school?"

The kid took another drag, then said, "Up yours, lady. I'm only four years old."

The young teacher of the fifth-grade class was disconcerted when Vinnie Gardella spent the first three days of the year staring at her. Finally, she asked him to stay after school and said, "Vincent, you've already fallen behind in your schoolwork. Is there any problem?"

"I'm in love," the boy replied.

"And who's the girl?" the teacher asked.

"It's you," Vinnie replied. "I can't stop thinking about you."

The young teacher blushed, then said, "Well, Vincent, I understand that everyone has dreams. I myself am looking forward to having a husband. But I don't want a child."

"That's okay, teach," the boy said. "I got a condom."

The boys were bragging in the grade-school playground. One boy announced proudly, "I know how babies are made."

"That ain't nothing," an Italian boy shouted. "I know how they aren't."

A group of little girls were playing when Angelo came by. One of the tots skipped over to him and asked, "Wanna play house?"

"Sure," Angelo replied. "Which one of you is gonna be the madam?"

What did the Italian teenager do when his date asked him to bring protection?
Picked her up with his three brothers.

How can you tell if a Boy Scout is Italian?
He walks old ladies halfway across the street.

Why don't flies buzz Italian children?
Even flies have some pride.

Did you hear about the ugly Italian baby?
His mother took the placenta home.

How can you tell a school is in a tough Italian neighborhood?
In biology class, they dissect a frogman.

The teacher said to the fourth-grade class, "Children, this is arts and crafts time. You can make anything you want."

A few minutes later, she walked around the room. Little Shirley was making a clay duck, little Mark was cutting out paper flowers, and little Jessica was coloring with crayons. The teacher was smiling with approval until she came to little Angelo, who was busy tearing the panties off little Joyce. "Angelo!" she screamed. "What in the world are you doing?"

He looked up at her and said, "Teach, you said we could make anything we want."

The teacher instructed her second-graders to come forward as their names were called and be prepared to draw something on the blackboard that was the cause of excitement in their homes the past week. One by one the pupils came forward and sketched such items as report cards, television sets, new clothes, a new baby, and other similar items. When the time came for Sophia to comply with the assignment, she walked to the board and drew two dots.

"What's that?" the puzzled teacher asked.

"Well," Sophia said, "the other day you told us that those dots are called periods."

"That's right," the teacher said. "But what could possibly be exciting about two periods?"

"I don't know," Sophia replied. "But that's how many my big sister says she missed, and everyone in my house started screaming."

Did you hear about the Italian kid whose teacher ordered the class to write a 200-word essay on what they did during summer vacation?
He wrote "Not much" 100 times.

A little Italian girl walked into the kitchen and asked, "Mama, do people go to heaven feetfirst?"

"Don't be silly," her mother replied. "Where did you get such an idea?"

"From Mrs. Donatello next door. When I looked in the window, I saw her lying on her bed with no clothes on. Her feet were up in the air and she was shouting, 'God, I'm coming. I'm coming.' It's a good thing Papa was on top of her holding her down."

CHAPTER 9

GREAT JOKES ABOUT DUMB ITALIANS

Why did the Italian plant Cheerios in his garden?
He wanted to grow donuts.

Why does the Italian army wear brown uniforms?
When they shit in their pants, it doesn't show.

What did the Italian do when he went into the pay toilet and read the sign DON'T PUT ANYTHING BUT TOILET PAPER INTO TOILET?
He shit on the floor.

Did you hear about the famous Italian plastic surgeon?
He repairs Tupperware.

What's the easiest job in the world?
A mind reader in Italy.

What did the Italian do when his wife complained about slack in the clothesline?
He moved his house.

How can you tell Italians from the other students?
Most students wear nametags; Italians wear VACANT signs.

Did you hear about the Italian who cut correspondence school?
He sent in empty envelopes.

Did you hear about the Italian engineer who invented a car that went 120 miles an hour without using a drop of gasoline?
It was called the Ronzoni Downhill.

An Italian guy walked into his neighborhood pizzeria and ordered a pie.

When it came out of the oven, the owner asked, "Hey, do you want this cut into four pieces or eight pieces?"

"Four," the Italian guy said. "I'll never be able to eat eight pieces."

Why did the Italian have a rack of empty wine bottles in his celler?
For his friends who didn't drink.

Did you hear about the Italian who won a gold medal at the 1988 Olympic Games?
He had it bronzed.

Did you hear about the Italian guy who couldn't spell?
He spent the night in a warehouse.

Why don't they ever give Italian workers more than a half hour for lunch?
It would take all afternoon to retrain them.

What Italian has an IQ of 165?
Sicily.

What's a bigamist to an Italian?
A dense fog.

What's bigotry to an Italian?
A very tall oak.

What do you call dirty poetry in Italian?
Vice versa.

What do those words mean that are stamped onto the bottom of every bottle of Italian wine?
"Open other end."

What's an Italian's favorite fast food?
Whoppers.

What did the Italian guy do when his wife asked him to get a can opener?
Came back with Ex-Lax.

What's a happy Roman?
Gladiator.

An Italian guy walked into a drugstore and asked for deodorant. "Certainly," the clerk replied. "Do you want the ball type?"
"No," the wop replied. "It's for under my arms."

Did you hear about the dumb Italian construction worker?
He wanted to take a day off, so he called in dead.

What's the definition of gross ignorance?
144 Italians.

How can you tell an Italian woman is dumb?
When she takes off her sweater to count to two.

The Italian girl was standing on the street when a man stopped and said, "Excuse me, doll, but did you know you have a tampon hanging out of your mouth?"

"Oh, my God!" she exclaimed. "What did I do with my cigarette?"

What's the definition of a dumb wop?
A guy who rolls up his sleeve when a girl says she wants to feel his muscle.

What did the Italian do when he found out he'd been promoted to the sixth grade?
He got so excited he cut himself shaving.

The wealthy couple hired an Italian caretaker to do some work around their estate while they toured Europe. A month later, they arrived home during a violent rainstorm. To their great horror, they walked into their living room to find the wop sitting in the middle of the floor while water poured from the ceiling.

"You idiot!" the man shouted. "I told you about that roof. Get up there right now and stop that leak."

"Can't," the Italian replied. "It's raining too hard."

"Well, why didn't you fix it when it wasn't raining outside."

"Because," the Italian replied, "it wasn't leaking then."

Why did the Italian burglar break two windows?
One to get in, and one to get out.

What's it called when you play a game of wits with an Italian?
Solitaire.

The boss called the Italian into his office and said, "Son, you're a hard worker. I want to enroll you in a course that tells you how to get ahead."
"I don't wanna go," the Italian replied.
"Why?" the boss asked.
"I already got a head."

What is an Italian jigsaw puzzle?
One piece.

Why did the horny Italian run to the department store?
He heard women's pants were half off.

Why did God make urine yellow and cum white?
So Italians would know if they were coming or going.

Why are Polish jokes so short?
So Italians can understand them.

Did you hear about the two Italians who froze to death in their car at a drive-in movie?
They went to see CLOSED FOR THE WINTER.

Vito had just arrived on the boat from Italy, and he was wandering the streets seeing the sights. He was passing a post office when he looked in the window and saw a poster that said WANTED FOR RAPE AND MURDER.
So he went in and applied for the job.

American ships are always easy to pick out because their names start with U.S.S., which stands for "United States Ship."
British ships are always easy to pick out, because their names start with H.M.S., which stands for "Her Majesty's Ship."
Italian ships are always easy to pick out, because their names start with A.M.B., which stands for "Atsa My Boat."

One guy said to another guy, "Hey, I like your shoes. What kind are they?"

His friend replied, "They're my Italian shoes."

"Italian shoes?"

"Yeah. Wherever I go, dago."

What's a titeria?
A brassiere factory in Italy.

What's "copulate"?
What the chief says to a police officer who walks in a half hour after he was supposed to start work.

What's an Italian diaphragm?
A wop stopper.

Miss Venturo was just hired as a nurses aide in the hospital. The head nurse gave her some instructions, then turned to consult with the doctor. A few minutes later, they turned to see a patient running out of his room, screaming in horrible pain while holding his crotch.

The head nurse took one look, then yelled, "Venturo! I told you to prick his boil."

CHAPTER 10

GREAT DISGUSTING ITALIAN JOKES

The woman sat up in bed and for the thousandth time and demanded, "Mario, why don't you ever go down on me?"

"Shut up and go to sleep."

"That's all you ever say. I want to know why you won't go down on me." She lifted up her nightgown and asked, "Is it because my cunt's not clean enough?"

"What?"

"I said, 'Is it because you don't think my cunt's clean enough?' "

"What?"

"Mario, are you deaf or something?" she screamed.

"Sorry," he replied. "The flies are buzzing so loud I can't hear you."

Gino staggered home drunk hours late. His wife sat in the kitchen, fuming. "I thought you were gonna take me out to dinner?" she demanded.

He replied, "I'll tell you what. How'd you like a large pizza with double cheese, double sausage, double pepperoni, and double anchovy."

"That sounds great," she replied.

So he leaned over and threw up in her lap.

The bereaved husband was standing by the casket in the funeral home, greeting the scores of relatives and friends who'd come to Palermo from as far as fifty miles away. Finally, his older brother came up to him and told him they had to talk in private. When they left the room, the older brother said, "Luigi, what's got into you? They can't stop talking about it. Why in the name of the holy virgin did you put her in a Y-shaped casket?"

"I had to," Luigi replied. "When I got home from work, she was in bed naked. For once she wasn't griping about a headache. So I took off my clothes and climbed on. By the time I noticed she was dead, I couldn't get her legs back together."

What's an Italian abortion?
Douching with Drano.

Why do they import Polish garbage into Italy?
They sell it as pizza topping.

Two guys were sitting at the bar talking about women. One guy said, "I've always been partial to blondes. But there's this Italian chick at work that I can't stop staring at."

His friend snorted. "Forget Italian women."

"Why?"

"They all got the exactlies."

"What in the hell are the exactlies?" the guy asked.

"You really want to know?"

"Yeah," the guy said.

The friend told him, "Put your hand in your pants and stick a finger up your ass."

"No way."

They argued for a moment, then the guy finally did as he was told.

The friend said, "Smell your finger."

The guy did it and winced. "So what does this have to do with the exactlies?"

"An Italian girl's cunt smells exactly like your finger."

A guy reported late for work one day at the pizzeria. The cashier said to him, "Hey, Tony, you look like shit. You feel okay?"

"Fine," Tony replied. He started up working when the other cook said, "Man, you look awful. You ought to see a doctor."

Tony again protested that he felt fine. But by lunchtime so many people had told him how terrible he looked that he started to get a little worried. Then the boss came by and said, "Tony, I can't take a chance on you infecting the customers. There's a doctor's office across the street. I insist you get yourself checked."

Tony protested, but a few minutes later he walked across the street and into the very dingy office of "Dr. Mocelli." The old Italian man who came out looked very crazy, but Tony was under strict orders to get himself checked. He told the old man what had happened.

"You are in luck," the old man said. "I just a got a new book of symptoms." He turned the pages slowly, mumbling to himself, "Looks bad, feels bad. Looks good, feels good. Looks good, feels bad—ah, here it is. Looks bad, feels good."

Tony said impatiently, "Tell me, doc. What do I have?"

"It says here," the doc said, "that if you look bad and feel good, you's a vagina."

Sophia was frustrated over her lousy sex life, so she talked to her next-door neighbor. The neighbor asked Sophia what she wore to bed.

"I have this white nightgown with a high lacy front and a low-cut back. Giorgio used to think it was sexy, but now he doesn't even look at me."

"Turn it around so it's cut low in front," the neighbor advised. "It's sure to turn Giorgio on."

That night, Giorgio climbed into bed and turned on the wrestling, as usual. Sophia went into the bathroom, put her nightgown on backward, moved seductively out the door and across the room, turned off the TV, got into bed, and nibbled on Giorgio's ear.

Giorgio just grunted and rolled over.

Sophia slapped him on the arm. "Giorgio, I want to make love," she said. "Don't you notice anything different about my nightgown?"

"Yeah," he said. "The shit stains are on the front."

Giuseppe couldn't get anywhere with girls because of his horrible breath. He went to his doctor for an exam. The doctor told him, "I'm afraid you need a psychiatrist instead."

"Why a psychiatrist?"

"You have to break one of your two bad habits—you either gotta stop scratching your ass or biting your fingernails."

What does an Italian call his nose?
A snack dispenser.

Why did the Italian get fired from his job cleaning toilets in a Las Vegas casino?
They caught him skimming off the top.

Why is an Italian woman like a pedophile?
They're both good at making babies.

The Italian guy considered himself God's gift to women. His macho attitude got him in a lot of trouble. One night he tried to pick up the girlfriend of a Mafia hoodlum in a singles bar, and a fight broke out. The next thing he knew, he woke up in a hospital bed. Although he was groggy and in pain, the first thing he noticed was the big tits of a nurse leaning over him. He reached up and squeezed them hard.

The nurse screamed and jumped back. "Don't do that!" she scolded.

"Come on, baby," the Italian said. "You've never had anyone like me. I know you want it."

The nurse grimaced in disgust. "No way, mac. If you're feeling horny, you'll just have to play with yourself."

The guy reached under the covers and found he was almost completely covered with bandages. "How can I do that?"

"Easy, Mr. Stud," the nurse replied. "Want to feel your organ?"

He nodded.

The nurse reached into a jar, pulled something out of formaldehyde, and said, "Here, catch."

An Italian man went to a doctor for a routine examination. When it was over, the doctor said, "You're in good shape, Mr. Margotti, but you've got the dirtiest balls I've ever seen."

Embarrassed, the man went straight home. When he walked in the front door, he called out, "Honey, come downstairs right away. I've got something I want to talk to you about."

His wife retorted, "I can't come and talk now. I'm so busy I don't even have time to wipe my ass."

Her husband replied, "That's what I have to talk to you about."

Why do an Italian's burps smell so bad?
They're farts that made a U-turn.

Why are Italian women like dogshit?
The older they get, the easier they are to pick up.

An Italian man and his wife went to the theater. Halfway through the movie, the wife turned and said, "Carmine, I gotta get up. My ass fell asleep."

Her husband snorted, "That's impossible. Your ass can't fall asleep."

The woman said, "I tell you, my ass fell asleep. I gotta get up."

The husband was about to protest again when a man in the seat behind them leaned forward and said, "I'll tell you, mac, her ass did fall asleep. It's been snoring ever since she sat down."

How do you know an Italian woman has bulimia?
After she eats, she sticks two fingers up her ass to shit it all out.

Why was the Italian hooker with VD so exhausted?
All she did was eat and run.

27 million Americans can't read a bedtime story to a child.

It's because 27 million adults in this country simply can't read.

Functional illiteracy has reached one out of five Americans. It robs them of even the simplest of human pleasures, like reading a fairy tale to a child.

You can change all this by joining the fight against illiteracy.

Call the Coalition for Literacy at toll-free **1-800-228-8813** and volunteer.

Volunteer Against Illiteracy. The only degree you need is a degree of caring.